TINA TURNER :
Beyond The
Spotlight

The inside of Tina Turner's journey in
overcoming
domestic violence and health issues, as
well as her comeback in the music
industry.

By

GREGORY P. MARTINS

Disclaimer

Table of content

CHAPTER 7

- Legacy and Influence Style and Musical Influence
- Feminist Icon and Empowerment
- Cultural Impact and Global Recognition
- Persevering through Ubiquity and Praises

Conclusion

Introduction

Tina Turner is a legendary American singer, songwriter, and performer who was born Anna Mae Bullock on November 26, 1939. Tina Turner is well-known for her powerful voice, dynamic stage presence, and electrifying performances. She has made a lasting impression on the music business. She has had a successful career spanning several decades, during which time she has faced personal and professional challenges, become an iconic figure, and become a cultural phenomenon.

Tina Turner's musical journey has been marked by resilience, reinvention, and an unwavering pursuit of excellence, from her early days as a member of the Ike & Tina Turner Revue to her groundbreaking solo career. Her capacity to enamor crowds with her heartfelt vocals and dynamic energy has cemented her status as one of the best performers ever.

In addition to her musical accomplishments, Tina Turner's life is a model of perseverance and resilience. She persevered through a wild and oppressive union with Ike Turner prior to tracking down the boldness to break free and secure herself as an independent craftsman. Because she exemplifies empowerment, resilience, and the power of self-belief, her personal triumphs and struggles have made her an inspiration to many, particularly women.

Tina Turner has made significant contributions through her activism and philanthropic work, in addition to her musical legacy. Her endeavors against illegal exploitation and the foundation of the Tina Turner Establishment mirror her obligation to have a constructive outcome on society and elevate those out of luck.

We delve into Tina Turner's early life and childhood, her remarkable musical journey, her personal life and relationships, her capacity to overcome personal and professional challenges, and her enduring legacy and influence in this comprehensive examination of her life and career. Through her story, we gain knowledge of the existence of a genuine symbol, whose effect on music and culture rises above age.

CHAPTER 1

Childhood and Early Life :Birth and Name

Tina Turner was born on November 26, 1939, in Nutbush, a small rural town in Haywood County, Tennessee, United States. Her birth name was Anna Mae Bullock. She was the little girl of Zelma Priscilla (née Currie) and Floyd Richard Bullock.

Tina spent her early years in Nutbush, Tennessee, a close-knit community where she developed a love for music and was surrounded by rhythm and blues, gospel, and blues music. She experienced the challenges and racial tensions of the time while growing up in a segregated South, which later influenced her activism and music.

Tina Turner's parents had a significant impact on her life and musical career. Zelma, her mother, was a strong, independent nursemaid who also worked in a factory. Floyd, her father, was a Baptist deacon who also sharecropped and worked in construction. Tina's musical style was shaped by her parent's love of music and involvement in the church, despite their divorce when she was young. They showed her powerful gospel performances and soulful melodies.

Tina's early musical interests

Tina showed a natural affinity for music from a young age. She was charmed by the exhibitions of craftsmen like B.B. Lord and Mahalia Jackson, whose records she paid attention to on her grandma's phonograph. Tina started singing when she was young, and she often performed in front of her family and friends to show off her new talent.

Instructive Foundation and Tutoring

Tina went to Flagg Forest School, an isolated school in Nutbush, where she accepted her initial training. In any case, her schooling was disturbed when her family moved to St. Louis, Missouri, looking for better open doors. In St. Louis, she proceeded with her schooling at

Sumner Secondary School, where she confronted provokes yet additionally tracked down potential chances to investigate her melodic capacities.

Difficulties and Challenges Confronted
Tina Turner confronted a few difficulties during her initial life. Cultural shifts and difficulties adjusting to a new environment came with moving from a rural town to an urban setting. Moreover, she encountered destitution, separation, and the difficulties of a wrecked home, which added to the versatility and assurance she would later show in her profession.

Tina's musical upbringing and development
Tina's talent continued to grow in St. Louis. She joined the school choir, where her talent was noticed by her music teacher, who saw potential in her. Tina also began performing, honing her stage presence and vocal skills, at local clubs and talent shows. Her future success as a singer

was built on the foundation of these early performances.

Transition to St. Louis, Missouri In 1956, when Tina Turner was 16 years old, her family moved to St. Louis. She was able to access a vibrant music scene and pursue her dreams thanks to this move, which proved to be a turning point in her life. Her rise from a small-town girl to a legendary music icon took place in St. Louis.

CHAPTER 2

Melodic Profession :Arrangement of Ike and Tina Turner Revue

Tina Turner's melodic profession took off when she met performer Ike Turner in 1957. Ike offered her a position as a backup singer in his band because he was impressed by her exceptional vocal ability. Before long, Tina's strong voice and energizing stage presence dazzled crowds, driving Ike to rebrand the gathering as the Ike and Tina Turner Revue. Tina turned into a fundamental piece of the band, displaying her dynamic exhibitions and adding to their special mix of R&B, soul, and rock 'n' roll.

Leap Forward and Achievement

During the 1960s, Ike and Tina Turner earned huge respect for their vivacious live exhibitions and hit records. They made famous songs like "A Fool in Love," "It's Gonna Work Out Fine," and "River Deep – Mountain High," which showed off Ike's arrangements and Tina's soulful voice. They became a sought-after act in the music industry due to their electrifying stage presence and chemistry.

Performance Profession

Notwithstanding the progress of Ike and Tina Turner, the couple confronted individual and expert difficulties, prompting their partition and resulting in divorce in 1978. After the split, Tina set out on a wonderful performance vocation. In 1984, she released her first solo album, "Private Dancer," after signing with Capitol Records. Thanks to hit singles like "What's Love Got to Do with It" and "Private Dancer," the album became hugely popular. Tina's powerful vocals and newfound artistic freedom earned her praise from critics and made her a solo superstar.

Through her performance profession, Tina delivered a few effective collections, including "Disrupt Each Guideline," "International

Concern," and "Most extravagant fantasies." Her capacity to convey sincerely charged exhibitions and her unrivaled stage presence kept on charming crowds around the world. Tina Turner solidified her position as one of the greatest performers in the history of music with her powerful voice, energetic dance moves, and iconic live performances.

CHAPTER 3

Personal Life and Relationships :Relationship with Ike Turner

Tina Turner's turbulent relationship with Ike Turner had a significant impact on her personal life. They got married in 1962, but their marriage was difficult and violent. Ike and Tina Turner were successful as a musical duo despite the difficulties. Be that as it may, Tina confronted physical and psychological mistreatment from Ike all through their relationship. She broke off her relationship with him in 1976 and filed for divorce in 1978 after enduring years of abuse. Tina's search for her own identity and independence after their divorce marked a turning point in her life and career.

Union with Erwin Bach

Following her separation from Ike Turner, Tina Turner tracked down affection and satisfaction in her relationship with Erwin Bach. The couple began dating during the 1980s and secured the bunch in a confidential function in July 2013 subsequent to being together for over 25 years. Erwin Bach, a German music executive, has been Tina's partner and a significant influence on her life and career. He has been a strong supporter of her. Their getting through relationship features a feeling of strength and friendship that Tina had yearned for after her past wild marriage.

Children and Family

Tina Turner is the mother of four children from a variety of relationships. She had her most memorable youngster, Craig Raymond Turner, in 1958, preceding her union with Ike Turner. Ronald Renelle Turner, Michael Turner, and Raymond Craig Turner were the three additional sons she later gave birth to. Raymond, unfortunately, died in 2018, which profoundly impacted Tina and her loved ones. Regardless of the difficulties of adjusting to her profession and individual life, Tina has consistently focused on her youngsters and family, appreciating the minutes enjoyed with them.

Tina Turner has maintained connections with her extended family in addition to her immediate family. She has stressed the significance of her family's love and support in her life, pointing out how they have assisted her in overcoming both personal and professional obstacles.

CHAPTER 4

Overcoming Obstacles in Professional and Personal Life :Domestic Violence and Divorce

Tina Turner's life was marked by significant personal obstacles, particularly her experience with domestic violence while she was married to Ike Turner. Her mental, emotional, and physical abuse had a negative impact on her health. Tina was able to overcome the challenges and leave the abusive relationship in 1976, at which point she filed for divorce in 1978. She was able to reclaim her life and pursue her dreams on her own terms because she took the courageous step of escaping the violence cycle.

Problems with Her Health and Her Comeback

Tina Turner also had problems with her health that could have hurt her career. She had multiple surgeries after being diagnosed with a life-threatening intestinal condition in the late 1980s. Tina had to put her music career on hold during this time so that she could focus on her recovery. Nonetheless, her resolute assurance and versatility impelled her towards a noteworthy rebound. She arose more grounded and got back to the stage with the arrival of her collection "International Concern" in 1989, which delivered hit singles like "The Best" and "Hot Windows." Tina Turner's victorious re-visitation to the music scene exhibited her capacity to defeat misfortune and recapture her legitimate spot in the business.

Tina Turner has encountered numerous personal and professional obstacles throughout her life; however, she has consistently demonstrated remarkable strength and resilience in overcoming them. Her capacity to transcend misfortune and remake her life and vocation fills in as a motivation to many, exhibiting the influence of constancy and assurance.

CHAPTER 5

Achievements and Awards : Grammy Awards

Tina Turner has received numerous awards, including multiple Grammy Awards, for her exceptional talent and contributions to the music industry. She won a total of 12 Grammy Awards throughout her career for her outstanding recordings and performances. "Proud Mary," "What's Love Got to Do with It," and "Better Be Good to Me" are among her notable Grammy-winning songs. Tina's Grammy wins length different classes, including Best Female Stone Vocal Execution, Best Female Pop Vocal Execution, and Best R&B Vocal Execution. She remains one of the most acclaimed and influential artists of her time thanks to her Grammy Awards.

Rock and Roll Hall of Fame

Tina Turner was inducted twice into the Rock and Roll Hall of Fame in recognition of her groundbreaking contributions to rock and roll music. First, she and her former husband, Ike Turner, were inducted into the band Ike & Tina Turner in 1991. This paid tribute to their significant collaborations and contributions to the music industry. In recognition of her remarkable solo career and her lasting influence on popular music, Tina was later inducted as a solo artist in 2021. Her induction into the Rock and Roll Hall of Fame is a testament to her significant impact on the rock and roll genre and her lasting legacy.

Kennedy Center Honors

In 2005, Tina Turner received the Kennedy Center Honors, one of the most prestigious awards in the performing arts. People who have made significant contributions to American culture through the performing arts receive this honor. Tina's inclusion on the prestigious Kennedy Center Honorees list demonstrates her immense talent, cultural impact, and lasting legacy as a performer, singer, and songwriter.

These are just a few examples of Tina Turner's accomplishments and awards; she has also been honored.

CHAPTER 6

Work Against Human Trafficking and Philanthropy :Tina Turner's Philanthropic Initiatives

Tina Turner has devoted her efforts to the fight against human trafficking. Having encountered individual difficulties in her day-to-day existence, including a troublesome marriage and conquering misfortune, she has been especially energetic about helping other people who have confronted comparative difficulties. Tina has supported organizations and initiatives that support victims' rescue, rehabilitation, and prevention of human trafficking by utilizing her platform and resources to raise awareness of the issue. Her dedication to this cause has significantly contributed to raising awareness of the plight of victims of human trafficking and promoting their rights and well-being.

Tina Turner Establishment

Laid out in 1993, the Tina Turner Establishment has been a critical generous undertaking of Tina Turner. The foundation's mission is to lend a hand to a variety of humanitarian endeavors, including initiatives related to health, education, and the arts and culture. Through her establishment, Tina has given monetary help to projects that advance training, give medical care benefits, and enable people and networks out of luck. The Tina Turner Foundation exemplifies her determination to make a positive impact on the lives of others and to use her success to encourage and assist those in need.

Tina Turner's activism and charitable work demonstrate her desire to have a significant impact beyond music. Her endeavors have helped bring issues to light and support for significant causes, motivating others to participate in the battle against social shameful acts and add to positive change.

CHAPTER 7

Legacy and Influence Style and Musical Influence

Tina Turner had an unimaginable impact on the music business, and her influence continues to resonate with musicians and fans all over the world. With her strong voice, charging stage presence, and vivacious exhibitions, Tina reclassified the limits of rock, soul, and R&B music. Her exceptional mix of profound vocals, enthralling dance moves, and crude energy put her aside as a genuine symbol. Specialists from different types have referred to Tina Turner as a wellspring of motivation, with her dynamic exhibitions and dauntless way to deal with music preparing people for the future of entertainers.

Feminist Icon and Empowerment

Tina Turner is a symbol of empowerment for women all over the world because of her personal journey of overcoming adversity and

her refusal to be defined by her past. Through her music and her own background, she exemplified strength, versatility, and the force of self-conviction. Numerous women have been inspired by Tina's fierce determination to forge her own path, achieve success on her terms, and embrace their individuality to courageously pursue their dreams. She broke down barriers and challenged conventional gender roles in the music industry, turning her into a feminist icon.

Cultural Impact and Global Recognition
Tina Turner is a global phenomenon because of her impact on cultures and borders. Her music has been embraced all over the world and resonated with people of all backgrounds. Tina's energizing exhibitions and enabling verses have associated with crowds on a general level, collecting her a monstrous worldwide fan base. Her impact stretches out past the domain of music, as she has turned into a social symbol, known for her unmistakable style, notable hair, and enthralling stage presence.

Persevering through Ubiquity and Praises

Indeed, even in the wake of resigning from the music business, Tina Turner's ubiquity stays solid. New generations of listeners continue to adore and celebrate her music. Her timeless hits, such as "What's Love Got to Do with It," "Proud Mary," and "Simply the Best," are still ingrained in popular culture. Numerous honors and awards have been given to Tina for her contributions to music and influence on popular culture. These include inductions into the Rock and Roll Hall of Fame, the Grammy Awards, and the Kennedy Center Honors. Her getting through inheritance is a demonstration of her uncommon ability, strength, and enduring impact.

Conclusion

Tina Turner's life and work demonstrate her remarkable talent, resilience, and strength. Tina has made a lasting impression on the music industry and popular culture, beginning with her time in the Ike & Tina Turner Revue and continuing with her groundbreaking solo career. She overcame obstacles, both personal and professional, such as an abusive marriage and health issues, demonstrating her unwavering spirit and determination.

Through her strong voice, zapping stage presence, and enabling verses, Tina Turner turned into a symbol of music, moving ages of craftsmen and fans. Tina's influence as a feminist icon and symbol of empowerment continues to resonate, encouraging individuals to embrace their individuality, overcome obstacles, and pursue their dreams fearlessly. Her boundary-breaking performances broke down barriers and redefined the rock, soul, and R&B genres.

Past her melodic accomplishments, Tina Turner's charity and activism have additionally set her inheritance. Her neutralizing illegal exploitation and the foundation of the Tina Turner Establishment exhibit her obligation to have a constructive outcome on society and elevate those out of luck.

A testament to her lasting influence and cultural significance is Tina Turner's numerous awards and recognitions, including her induction into the Rock and Roll Hall of Fame, Grammy Awards, and Kennedy Center Honors.

The story of Tina Turner is one of triumph, perseverance, and inspiration. Her journey serves as a reminder that even the most difficult obstacles can be overcome with perseverance, bravery, and a strong spirit, resulting in a lasting legacy of greatness. Tina Turner will always be remembered as an icon and true musical legend who has touched the lives of millions of people worldwide.

.